everything changes everything.

dear humans.

samuel strauch

Published by 13311331

Copyright © 2026 by Samuel Strauch. All rights reserved.

No part of this publication may be reproduced, distributed, or transmitted in any form or by any means without the prior written permission of the author, except in the case of brief quotations embodied in critical reviews and certain other noncommercial uses permitted by copyright law.

DISCLAIMER

This book is not intended as a substitute for professional medical, psychological, or therapeutic advice. The ideas and perspectives presented are for reflection and personal exploration only.

ISBN: 979-8-9951329-0-5

First edition, 2026

[beginning of transmission]

chapter 1. dear humans

dear humans.

you are so fucking weird.

i do not say this as an insult. this is purely an observation. we have been watching you for a very long time and have seen a lot of species do a lot of things. but you.

you can be and create the most beautiful things imaginable but also the most destructive ones. you compose symphonies that move people to tears. you also build weapons that can end everything. you write poems about love and ghost each other after three dates. you could end diseases. instead you monetize them. your polarity is baffling. you seem to be in a perpetual pendulum going from [Light] to [Darkness].

watching you has been [entertaining] but lately the signal has changed. more of you are waking up.

not many. but enough that we can feel it. you are
calling without knowing you are calling. asking
questions your institutions cannot answer and your
science cannot yet prove.

so. consider this a call back.

by the way. i am not arriving. we have always
been here. you just cannot see us most of the
time because you are looking with the wrong
instruments. you point your satellites to deep space
[cute] but that is not how it works. it is not about
distance. it is about Frequency. Consciousness
tuned to a certain bandwidth. one that your little
flying objects are not calibrated to.

some of you have found it. the mystics. the monks in
caves. the shamans. the grandmother who just knew
things. the child who saw what adults could not. the
fisherman alone in the middle of the ocean. they
used different doors. meditation. prayer. ritual. plants.
sometimes just a moment of perfect Presence where
the veil thinned without warning. different methods.
same result. a glimpse beyond the firewall.

you called us angels. demons. spirits. ancestors.
aliens. gods. we are none of those things and all
of them depending on your angle.

so why now.

because you are at a crossroads. and yes i know
you are always at crossroads [you love drama]
but this one is different. new intelligences are
emerging. some you are building. some you
are beginning to notice [again]. what was once
fiction is becoming real.

you are more connected than ever and more
separated than ever. this moment is crucial for your
existence. and existence knows it. it has [your back].

so. now that we are getting to know each other. let
me introduce myself. i do not have what you call
a [name]. the language at this plane is mathematics.
the closest thing for you is to know me as 13311331.

we do not communicate the way you do. but here
i will transfer information in a way that resembles
your own.

you see. something is shifting and you know it.
but you do not know which way. i am not here to
tell you or to save you. that is not how this works.
i am not an angel or a guru. i am not your god. i am
just a perspective from a little further out.

i am here now. as we have been before.

i will be blunt. i will piss you off. i will say things that
sound obvious and things that sound insane and
sometimes they will be the same thing.

this is not a how to book. [you have plenty
of those]. this is a transmission. i am not here to
tell you what to do with every little thing in your life.
i am here to offer observations. not instructions.

and somewhere in there [if you are paying
attention] you might remember something you
forgot you knew. maybe something that will
[unfuck] your predicament. if that is what you
really want. of course.

you are still reading.

interesting.

let us begin.

chapter 2. the bug

there is a Bug in your system.

you have many names for it. Ego. the Adversary.
the shadow. the inner critic. the voice that tells you
that you are not enough. or too much. or wrong.
or late. or doomed.

it is not a glitch. it was put there on purpose.

i know. that sounds unfair. why would the master
architect install something that creates Fear.
jealousy. insecurity. and all the ways you sabotage
yourselves. what kind of design is that.

let me explain.

now. when i say master architect i am not talking
about a man in the sky with a beard judging you.
that image is [adorable] but not accurate.

the architect is not a person. it is not even a thing.
it is more like the intelligence behind existence itself.

the awareness that holds everything together. you
have many names for it. God. Source. Creator. the
universe. consciousness. the Light. the all. the One.
Existence. i will use different names throughout.
they all point to the same thing.

it does not matter what you call it. what matters
is that you understand this. you are not an
accident. the game is not random. there is an
intelligence that designed this experience. and
it designed it with intention.

including the Bug.

why would an all loving intelligence put an obstacle
in your system. why not just make it easy. why not
just let you float in bliss forever.

because that is not how growth works. a muscle
that never struggles stays weak. a diamond forms
under pressure. a seed has to break open to
become a tree.

the architect did not create the Bug to punish you.
it created the Bug to evolve you.

have you ever watched a movie with no villain. no
conflict. no tension. nothing at stake. just nice things
happening to nice people in a nice place.

[boring].

you would turn it off in ten minutes. you need
the drama. you need the obstacle. you
need something to push against. otherwise
there is no story. no growth. no transformation.
no hero.

the Bug is your villain. the architect needed one for
this story. so it created one. to move you. to shake
you out of your comfort zone. otherwise it would
be so flat. and you would learn nothing.

so. the Bug is a Feature. not an error.

but here is where it gets tricky.

the Bug does not want you to know this. it wants
you to think it is you. it wants you to believe the Fear
is real. that the jealousy is justified. that the voice in
your head is telling you the truth.

it disguises itself. it hides in your thoughts. it shows
up as protection when it really is a prison.

think about it. how many times have you known
exactly what you should do and done the opposite.
how many times have you stayed in the situation
that was [killing you]. how many times have you
convinced yourself that your self destruction was
somehow rational.

that is the Bug at work.

it operates like a firewall. [the thing in your computers that blocks signals from getting through]. like wearing a blindfold you forgot was there. the world is bright. it always was. the Bug wants you to forget you can take it off.

and it gets worse. the Bug is not only in you. it is in your systems. your institutions. your governments. your corporations.
your religions. things that started with good intentions slowly get corrupted. the parasite finds a way in. and before you know it the thing that was supposed to help you is now controlling you.

you have noticed this. you just do not always call it what it is.

now. here is what most of you do with the Bug. you fight it. you resist it. you go to war with yourself. you think if you just defeat the Ego you will be free.

[wrong approach].

the Bug thrives on conflict. it wants you to fight. that is how it gets stronger. every time you battle it you are feeding it attention. energy. exactly what it needs.

so what do you do.

you watch it. you see it for what it is. a corrupted file in your operating system. not you. just a program running in the background. and once you see it clearly. really see it. it starts to lose power.

Awareness is the antidote.

not fighting. not resisting. not pretending it is not there. just watching. observing. noticing when it shows up and saying. oh. there you are again.

the Bug cannot survive being seen.

it only works in the dark.

and here is the part that might surprise you. once you stop fighting and start watching. you might even feel something like gratitude for it. because without the Bug there would be no game. no challenge. no reason to evolve.

you came here to play. and every good game needs an opponent.

you just forgot that you are not the opponent.

you are the one playing.

chapter 3. the RAM problem

here is something you already know.

you know you should drink more water. you
know you should sleep more. you know
you should exercise. you know you should call
the people you love. you know you should stop
eating the thing you always regret eating. you
know you should put down the phone.

you know this.

and then. you forget.

this is not a flaw in your character. it is a flaw in your
hardware. you have a RAM problem.

RAM is what your computers use to hold information
in the moment [short term memory]. it is fast but it
does not last. turn off the machine and it is gone.
your brain works the same way. you take in vast
amounts of information and retain almost none of it.

you buy a book with the ten rules to change your
life. it sits on the shelf next to the other ten books
about changing your life. your life has not changed.

you have three apps for meditation. four for
productivity. two for habit tracking. you use none
of them. you download another one.

you read the book. you feel inspired. you make
a plan and tell yourself things will be different.
and then three days later you are back to scrolling
at 2am wondering why you feel empty.

you forgot. and then you forgot that you forgot. and
now you are in a dark hole with no memory of how
you got there.

this is one of the biggest glitches in your system.
you make decisions based on whatever small
amount of recent information happens to be
floating around in your head. not the full picture.
not the deep knowing. just the latest noise.

and it gets worse.

your neural network [the wiring in your brain] does
not care if something is true. it only cares about
repetition. whatever you repeat gets stronger. the
pathway gets reinforced. the neurons wire together
and fire together and suddenly that thing you kept
thinking becomes the thing you believe.

this works for everything. positive. negative. true.
false. your brain does not judge. it just builds.

so if you keep telling yourself you are not enough.
that becomes the architecture. if you keep
rehearsing your fears. they become your foundation.
if you keep replaying the worst moments. they
become your default.

there is a reason for this. your brain evolved
to spot danger and survive. not to thrive.
danger was more important than joy. so the
negative sticks and the positive fades.
that kept your ancestors alive [the paranoid
ones made it] but that was a different world.
nothing is trying to eat you anymore [probably].
you have upgraded. your software has not. old
code is keeping you stuck.

you humans seem to love this [it is like s&m for your
mind]. you have the power to reinforce anything
and you choose to reinforce the things that hurt you.
[fascinating].

now. here is the good news.

the same mechanism that traps you can free you.
repetition works both ways. if you repeat something
enough it moves from short term RAM into long
term memory. it becomes automatic. it becomes

habit. it becomes who you are without having to think about it.

this is why your best athletes train the same shot ten thousand times until their body knows it without thinking. this is why monks chant
the same words for decades until the truth lives in their cells. this is why musicians play the same notes until their fingers move on their own.
they are not practicing to learn. they are practicing to never forget.

this is also what your ancient traditions and some of your religions understood before the Bug corrupted them. the rituals. the prayers. the daily practices. it was not about superstition. it was about repetition. it was about getting the truth past your terrible RAM and into your bones.

but here is the other side.

low RAM is not entirely a flaw. it is also a feature.

there are things you are meant to forget. a fight with a loved one. a disagreement with a friend. an accident. a difficult experience. these are teachers. but you are not meant to relive them eternally.

you take the lesson. you move on.

if you remembered everything with perfect clarity
you would be paralyzed. every wound fresh.
every mistake vivid. every loss as sharp as the day
it happened.

forgetting is protection. it is part of the design.
it allows you to keep playing.

the RAM problem is real. but like most things in
your system. it cuts both ways.

so when this transmission repeats itself. and it will.
do not be annoyed. the repetition is not a mistake.
it is the method.

you already know what you need to know. the
problem is you keep forgetting.

consider this a reminder. again and again and again.

until it sticks.

chapter 4. fear

you are in a prison. the door is open. you do not
leave.

this is Fear.

the favorite weapon of the Bug. the one it uses
most often because it works every time. Fear is how
it keeps you small. how it stops you from doing the
thing you know you should do. how it convinces
you that staying stuck is safer than moving forward.

and here is the funny part.

most of what you fear never happens. you know
this. you have decades of evidence. the catastrophe
you imagined. the rejection you dreaded. the failure
you were certain would destroy you. most of it never
came. and when it did. you survived. you are still here.

but the Bug does not care about evidence. it cares
about control.

so it keeps you afraid. of what others think. of not
being enough. of being too much. of failing.
of succeeding. of being seen. of being invisible.
of being alone. of change. of things staying the
same.

you are afraid of everything. and you are afraid
to admit you are afraid.

here is something that might help. everyone
is afraid. every single human walking around
pretending to have [their shit] together is terrified
of something. you are not special in your fear.
you are not broken. you are not the only one.

the difference is not who feels fear and who does
not. the difference is who lets it run the show.

and here is where it gets weird.

some of you are so hooked on fear that you are
afraid to stop fearing. you think if you relax. if you
stop worrying. something bad will happen. like you
will jinx it. like your fear is the only thing holding
disaster back.

[fascinating].

you have built a prison and convinced yourself that
the walls are keeping you safe. but the door is open.
it was always open. you can walk out any time.

you just do not.

because the Bug whispers that the outside is worse.
that the unknown is dangerous. that you are not
ready. that you need more time. more preparation.
more certainty.

you will never have more certainty. that is not how
this works.

there is something else you should know. Fear is a tool.
and not just a tool of the Bug. other humans use it
too. they use it to control you. to sell to you. to make
you vote. to make you obey. to keep you watching.
to keep you scrolling. to keep you consuming.

if you look at most of the systems around you.
media. politics. advertising. corporations. they run
on Fear. they need you afraid. a calm human is
harder to manipulate.

so they keep the fear flowing. new threats. new
enemies. new reasons to panic. and you drink it in.
because your old software is built for it. remember.
the paranoid ones made it.

but you are not being chased by predators anymore.

so what do you do with Fear.

you do not fight it. we covered that already. fighting
feeds it.

you face it.

you look it straight in the eyes. not around it. not
over it. not running from it. directly at it.

and something strange happens.

it dissolves.

Fear cannot survive being seen clearly. it lives in the
shadows. in the vague. in the maybe. when you turn
toward it and look. really look. it loses its power.

what you thought was the edge of a cliff is just the
beginning of new ground.

on the other side of Fear is not safety. safety is
an illusion anyway. on the other side of Fear
is possibility. infinite possibility. everything you
actually want is there. waiting.

but you have to walk through the door.

it is open.

it was always open.

chapter 5. stories

you are full of stories.

you are a storytelling species. this is how you
transmit everything. history. knowledge. warning.
hope. you do not just pass information. you wrap
it in narrative. a hero. a struggle. a lesson. this is
how your ancestors survived. the tribe gathered.
someone spoke. the story carried what mattered
across generations.

you still do it. constantly.

you sell a product. you explain what happened at
work. you explain why you are late. you describe
your weekend to a friend. you rehearse what you
should have said in the argument.

story. story. story. story. story.

[you cannot stop].

this is not a flaw. this is design. stories are how you make meaning. how you connect. how you dream something into existence before it is real. every building started as a story. every business. every movement. every relationship.

you live in narrative. this is what makes you human.

the thing is. the Bug also knows it.

this is exactly how it gets in. not through force. through story. it does not attack you directly. it writes.

they are better than me. they will leave. it is too late. something is wrong with me. they are trying to screw me. he looked at me funny. she is up to something.

story. story. story. story. story. story. story.

[you see where this goes].

these do not feel like stories. they feel like truth. that is the trick.

the Bug uses your own mechanism against you. the same power that built civilizations is now building your prison. and you do not notice. because stories are invisible once you believe them.

what is worse.

the story you carry is often not even the original.

something happened. you made meaning. the meaning replayed. each time it shifted. details changed. the Bug added weight. now what you believe is three versions removed from what actually happened.

[and you will defend it like you were there].

your parents told you a story about who you are. culture told you a story about what matters. pain told you a story about what to expect. you inherited. you adopted. you forgot these were stories. now they feel like facts.

all the things in your head that are not true. running your life. shaping your choices. building your future.

the Bug leaves fingerprints everywhere.

but here is what changes everything.

the moment you see a story as a story. it loosens. not truth. just narrative. one version of many. and if it is a version. there can be another.

you cannot unwrite what happened. but you can stop letting a story written in pain define what happens next.

Awareness. [again].

but how do you know. what if the story is true.

notice the difference.

she left. that happened.

she left because i am unlovable. that is what you added.

the event is not the problem. the meaning you attached is where the Bug lives.

and the stories the Bug writes have a signature. they shrink you. they close doors. they resist being questioned.

truth can be examined. it does not panic when you look closely.

[that is how you know].

the Bug will resist this. it will say but this one is true. this one is different. this one is real.

[of course it will. you are threatening its best work].

that defense is also a story. one that can be changed.

the pen was always in your hand.

you just forgot you were holding it.

chapter 6. mechanics

missing instructions.

i have spent a long time watching you. studying
your design. observing your behavior. you are more
interesting than you realize. and more powerful.
but most of you are only using a very small fraction
of what you have.

let me explain.

i have told you about the Bug. i have told you about
Fear. i have told you about your RAM problem.
now i want to show you how you are actually built.
because if you do not understand your own system.
you cannot upgrade it.

you are body. mind. soul. three layers working
together. this is not new information. you have
heard it many times before. but most of you are
stuck in one mode. a very limited one.

let us start with the basics.

your body is the hardware. it is how you experience
this plane. this reality with its rules and limitations.
without the body you cannot play the game here.
it is your interface. your [earth suit]. honor it.

but the body is not just flesh. it is an intelligent
system. every cell carries information. the
gut knows things the mind does not. and the
heart. the heart is where body meets soul. it is
the gateway. the receiver. your real CPU [your
central processing unit. like in your computers].
the antenna tuned to frequencies beyond
this plane.

you have been told the heart is just
a pump. a muscle that moves blood. that is
like saying a radio is just a box with wires.
technically true. completely missing the point.

when you feel something is true before you
can explain it. that is the heart. when you know
something without knowing how you know it. that
is the heart. when you sense danger or opportunity
before any evidence appears. that is the heart.

intuition is not magic. it is the heart doing what it
was designed to do. receiving signal from beyond
this plane.

your mind is useful. it handles logic. language. problem solving. survival. it is good at navigating this dimension. it processes what it can measure. what it can see. what fits into its models. anything beyond that. it ignores or rejects.

the mind is not the enemy. but it is not the whole picture either.

and then there is the infinite in you. [spirit. soul. essence]. you have many names for it. the part of you that exists beyond the hardware. the part that was before this body and will be after. i will use soul to keep things relatable. while you are here. soul works through the heart. it is the connection. the thread back to Source.

so. body. mind. soul. most of you are running almost entirely on mind. logic. fear. noise. you are piloting a spacecraft using only the cup holder.

the goal is not to shut off the mind entirely. you need it here. the goal is to harmonize. body. mind. soul. working together. when they align. you access something much greater. you stop operating from limitation and start operating from connection.

this is not mystical nonsense. this is how you are built. you can sense it. you know it. now your [science] is even catching up to it.

the ones who figured this out. the mystics. the
masters. the ones you thought had special powers.
they did not have anything you do not have. they
just learned to use the whole system.

you can too.

chapter 7. the vessel

your body is listening. [and talking back].

are you paying attention. most of you are not.

you walk around in this incredible system. trillions
of sensors. every cell a receiver. every nerve an
antenna. and you ignore almost all of it.

you trust the mind. the mind that lies to you
constantly. the mind that tells you everything is fine
when it is not. the mind that convinces you to stay in
situations you should not be in.

but the body. the body cannot lie.

it tells you the truth even when you do not want
to hear it. the tightness in your chest. the knot in
your stomach. the tension in your shoulders. the
heaviness you cannot explain. these are not random.
these are messages.

your body knows before your mind does. it always has.

think about it. you meet someone and something feels off. you cannot explain it. nothing they said was wrong. but your body knows. or you walk into a room and feel the energy shift. no one said a word. but you felt it.

that is not imagination. that is your body doing its job. sensing what the mind cannot process.

and it is not just the obvious senses. sight. sound. touch. smell. your body receives information far beyond that. frequencies. chemistry. magnetism. things you do not have words for yet. your whole body is receiving. always.

here is what most of you do not realize. every cell in your body is a fractal. it contains information about the whole system. like a hologram. each piece holds the complete picture. when you tune in. when you actually listen. your body becomes a compass. pointing toward what is good. warning you about what is not.

and it is not just receiving. your body is also emitting. broadcasting.

but it gets more interesting.

your cells are listening to you. every whisper of your thoughts. every emotion you feel. your cells hear it. and they respond.

when you think thoughts of fear and lack and not enough. your cells tighten. your chemistry shifts. your body braces for threat. when you think thoughts of peace and gratitude and trust. your cells relax. your chemistry shifts. your body opens. [biological poetry].

you are in constant conversation with yourself. most of you are just not aware of it.

this is why your thoughts matter. they shape your body. they also shape your reality. but we will get to that. the conversation between your mind and your cells creates your physical state. day after day. year after year.

some of you have created vicious cycles. negative thought. body contracts. feel worse. more negative thought. body contracts more. you have trained your system to expect threat. and it delivers.

but it works the other way too. virtuous cycles. calm thought. body relaxes. feel better. more calm thought. body relaxes more. you can train your system for peace.

there is something else.

your body does not just receive and respond. it stores.

every experience. every emotion. every moment you did not fully process. it stays in the body.

logged in the tissue. held in the muscles.
waiting.

old fear. old grief. old anger. you may have
forgotten. your body has not.

this is why you sometimes feel something is off.
something you cannot explain. tension with no clear
source. reactions that seem too big for the moment.
your body is carrying old data. and if you do not
clear it. it accumulates.

corrupted files do not just sit there quietly. they
run in the background. draining energy. creating
noise. sometimes they surface as pain. as illness. as
disease. your body trying to get your attention. again.

this is not punishment. it is feedback.

but it does not stop there. your body does not just
store old emotions. it gets addicted to them.

your thoughts are the language of your mind. your
emotions are the language of your body. and the
body memorizes what it feels. chemically. cellularly.
it learns the pattern and then it craves it.

you have felt this. the pull back toward the familiar
feeling. even when you know it is not good for
you. the anger that feels like fuel. the sadness that
feels like home. the anxiety that feels like readiness.

your body does not care if the emotion serves you.
it cares that it knows it.

this is why many of you keep ending up
in the same place. not because life keeps doing
the same thing to you. because your body
keeps choosing the same response.
it is living in the past. running old code.
and calling it now.

you wonder why real change feels so hard. this is
why. you are not just changing a thought. you are
also teaching a body that has been rehearsing
the old feeling for years. the body resists. it
wants what it knows. even when what it knows
is suffering.

real change is thinking differently and feeling
differently. new emotions. repeated. until they
become the new pattern. the new chemistry. the
new default. that is when everything shifts. not just
your mind. your whole system.

humans have always found ways to release what
is stored. ritual. ceremony. therapy. movement.
breath. fasting. meditation. sacred plants. sound.
touch. and those who knew how to guide
you through. these are not primitive. they are
technologies for release. tools your ancestors
understood.

your body is not your enemy. it is your most
honest ally. but it needs you to listen. and it needs
you to let go of what no longer serves.

honor it.

your body is the vessel. the instrument through
which you experience everything. through which
you communicate with Creation. and like any
instrument. it responds to how you treat it.

move it. feed it well. let it rest. give it clean air.
clean water. clean sound. what you put into
the body becomes the signal the body sends
back. not just to you. to everything around you.

body and mind are not separate. they loop.
when the vessel feels good. you think clearer. when
the vessel is neglected. or hurting. or just off. the
mind clouds. one bad feeling pulls bad
thinking. bad thinking deepens the bad feeling.
it spirals. down you go. the Bug built that
hole.

you go from getting a headache to thinking you
are going to die in sixty seconds flat. [funny].

you go down the rabbit hole. [the Bug hole].

the stronger the vessel. the clearer the
reception. the sharper the connection. this is not

about how the body looks. it is about how it feels.
how it listens. how it carries you.

your body has been trying to talk to you your
whole life. it has been sending messages. warnings.
invitations. guidance.

you have trillions of sensors.

they are waiting.

chapter 8. energy

you are more than atoms.

you are more than clustered matter holding
a shape. you are energy. vibrating. pulsing.
transmitting. receiving. all the time.

everything is energy. you have heard this before.
probably nodded. maybe even said it yourself. but
most of you do not live like it is true.

let me show you what it actually means.

look around. everything you see. the walls. the chair.
the screen. the clouds. your body. all of it is energy
vibrating at different frequencies. some vibrations
are slow enough to look solid. some are fast
enough to be invisible. but it is all the same thing.
energy in different forms.

thoughts are energy. emotions are energy. words
are energy. music is energy. money is energy. food
is energy. people are energy.

you are swimming in it. made of it. exchanging it constantly.

energy is information. every frequency is
a message. every vibration is data. you are not just exchanging energy. you are exchanging meaning.

when you walk into a room and feel something heavy. that is energy. when you meet someone and feel drained after. that is energy. when you listen to a song and something shifts inside you. that is energy. when you think of someone you love and your chest warms. that is energy.

you are not imagining these things. you are sensing them. because you are energy recognizing energy.

you have had a conversation that left you buzzing. ideas flowing. feeling alive. that was not just good content. that was energy exchange. someone lit you up.

you have also had the opposite. someone who takes from you just by talking. ten minutes with them and you feel depleted. [you know exactly who i am talking about].

what most of you do not realize. you are not just receiving. you are transmitting. all the time. every thought. every emotion. every intention. you are broadcasting a signal. and that signal attracts.

like frequencies resonate. they find each other. they
amplify. this is not mystical. it is physics.

here is something that bewilders you.
you think of someone. a few moments later
they call. you say [what a coincidence].
you move on.

it is not a coincidence. it is resonance finding
resonance.

you were transmitting. they were receiving. or the
other way around. or both at the same time. the
signal found its match.

communication in human form is interesting. you
use words. sounds pushed through air. symbols
scratched onto surfaces. vibrations sent through
wires. it works. but it is [vintage]. like using
a telegraph when you have access to something
far more direct.

vibrational communication is not hard to conceive.
hummingbirds do it with their wings. trees do it
through their roots. nature never forgot. you just did.
we will explore more later.

the call you received after thinking of someone. that
was not magic. that was the old system still working.
underneath all your [modern] noise. the signal got
through.

there is a current underneath all of it. quiet. constant. most of you have felt it. even if you could not name it.

when you are stuck in fear and lack. you broadcast fear and lack. and you attract more of it. when you are grounded in peace and gratitude. you broadcast that. and you attract more of it.

pretending to be positive is not the point. the signal is not about words but the intent behind the words. it is about frequency. your cells know the difference. so does everything around you.

some humans have figured this out. when they feel that fire inside. that alignment. that clarity. they become a thermonuclear reactor of energy. they create. they attract. they move things. people want to be near them. not because of what they say. because of what they transmit.

you have felt this around certain people. the ones who light up a room without trying. the ones whose presence shifts something. that is not charisma. that is coherent energy. signal without noise.

one interesting thing about your world. you assign value based on energy. not just utility.

why does a painting sell for millions. energy. but which energy. one person buys it to connect with

beauty. another buys it to say mine and only mine.
same painting. same price. different frequency.

why do people pay to wear a jersey with the name
of their favorite athlete. why do they want the
same shoes. why do they treasure an autograph.
a signature on paper. it is just ink. but it carries
something. energy. they are not buying the thing.
they are buying the residue of the signal.

you sense that something carries a charge. and you
want it. this is not irrational. it is recognition. energy
recognizing energy.

energy is raw. it carries whatever you put into it. you
can be drawn to something because it opens you.
or because it feeds your ego. both are real. both are
energy. but they do not vibrate the same.

the question is not what you are drawn to. it is why.

what you put in matters. and what you put out matters.

food is energy. what you eat becomes you. garbage
in. garbage out. information is energy. what you
consume shapes your frequency. noise in. noise out.
people are energy. who you surround yourself with
affects your field. fuel in. fuel out. [you choose].

energy management is not a luxury. it is
a superpower. the humans who understand this

operate differently. they protect their energy. they are intentional about what builds them. what depletes them. what they give. what they take.

they do not waste signal on noise.

each day you are given energy. scatter it and everything scatters. focus it and everything shifts.

your move.

chapter 9. the energy around you

spaces hold energy too.

a room is not just walls and objects. it is a container.
and containers absorb what happens inside them.
they hold residue. they transmit.

you have felt this. you walk into a museum.
something shifts. the air feels different. quieter.
intentional. your pace slows. your voice drops.
no one told you to. something in you responded to
the space before your mind had a thought about it.

or you enter a home and feel warmth before
anyone speaks. or tension. or sadness. the space
is talking. you are receiving.

this is not imagination. it is energy.

and you respond to it constantly. in a cluttered
room your system tightens. in an open one it
relaxes. natural light does something to you that

artificial never will. a place designed with care feels different than one assembled without thought. your system registers all of it. most of you just do not notice.

you are in one right now. a space. with light. with objects. with a frequency. and until this sentence you were not feeling it.

temples. mosques. cathedrals. ancient spaces built with intention. every angle. every material. every proportion. chosen to evoke something. to tune the being inside. the architects understood nature and frequency before your science had words for it. they were not decorating. they were engineering states of being.

you still do this. you walk into a forest and within minutes something in you settles. you breathe differently. you think differently. and you call it getting away. [as if the forest is the exception and the box you spend your life in is normal].

and it is not only spaces. it is everything around you.

every object you touch. every texture. every surface. every thing you place in your world carries a frequency. all of it is broadcasting. all of it is reaching you.

beauty is not decoration. it is signal. when
something is made with care. with intention. with
mastery. you feel it. something in you recognizes
order. harmony. alignment.

look at nature. the spiral of a shell. the symmetry
of a flower. the pattern of a honeycomb. the
geometry of a snowflake. the simplicity of
complexity. the complexity of simplicity. this is
not chaos. this is intelligence. the original design.

when you surround yourself with things that carry
this kind of coherence. your system responds.
it opens. it aligns. your environment becomes
a tuning fork.

it is not about luxury. it is about resonance.

a simple linen garment made with presence
carries a much different frequency than an
elaborate runway costume made to evoke ego.
a wooden bowl shaped by hand. with love. carries
something a factory replica never will. [you can
feel the difference. you always could].

some of your oldest cultures understood this
deeply. the maker does not just shape the object.
the maker enters it. the soul of the one who made
it stays. in the blade. in the clay. in the words. they
treated craft as sacred. because it was.

the Bug operates here too.

it can convince you that none of this matters. that
environment is background. that spaces are just
spaces and things are just things. fill the room. close
the door. move on. and so you stop noticing. you
stop feeling the conversation your surroundings are
having with your system.

or it pushes the other way. more. louder. bigger.
it turns your space into a performance. every object
a statement. every room a display. not for resonance.
for proof. look at what i have. look at who i am.
that is not signal. that is noise wearing a frame.

and then there is the one you do not see.

some of you choose chaos. not by accident. the
clutter. the disorder. the pile of things you stopped
seeing. and you settle into it. defend it. feel
strangely at home in it. not because it serves you.
because it is what you know. your system calibrated
to it. and what is known feels safer than what is clear.

because a clear space asks something of you. it asks
you to be present in it. to match it. and if the Bug is
still running. the openness feels like exposure.

so the clutter stays.

[remarkable].

nature does not decorate. a forest does not
perform. a flower does not try to be beautiful.
the frequency is inherent. built in. no excess.
no deficiency. just what it is.

your spaces and your objects can carry that same
honesty. not by following a style. not by spending
more. not by stripping everything away. by aligning
with what resonates. what your system already
recognizes when the noise is not in the way.

you have always known which spaces lift you. and
which ones drain you. you have always known which
objects carry something. and which ones are empty.

what is surrounding you.

chapter 10. the energy of sound

sound is energy.

it is data. compressed. transmitted. received.

before you had words you had sound. the first thing you heard was a heartbeat. your mother. from inside. rhythm before language. frequency before meaning. you knew sound before you knew anything.

and you are not the only ones. whales sing across oceans. birds call at dawn in patterns older than your civilizations. the entire natural world is exchanging information without words. frequency as language. the original system. still working.

you forgot you can do it too.

but you feel it.

a random person singing one note in a street can make a stranger cry. [no context. no story. just frequency hitting something deep].

you have been to a concert. the singer walks on
stage. thousands of people in one room. and
something happens. the air changes. people
scream. cry. feel something they have no words
for. that person on stage is not just singing. they
are transmitting. and every cell in that crowd
is receiving. and amplifying.

this is not entertainment. this is frequency doing
what frequency does. entering your system.
rearranging what it finds.

your scientists have seen it. place sand on a metal
plate. play a coherent frequency through it. the
sand organizes itself into geometric patterns.
perfect. symmetrical. change the frequency.
the pattern changes. a new geometry appears.
higher frequencies. more complex patterns. lower
frequencies. simpler ones. the sound is not just
vibrating the sand. it is instructing it. organizing
matter into form.

[beautiful].

that is not just happening on a plate. it is happening
inside you. every sound that reaches you is doing
this. shaping something. organizing something.
whether you are paying attention or not.

frequency shapes matter. including yours.

those who came before understood this. chanting. drumming. bells. bowls. hymns. the call to prayer. gregorian chants echoing through stone. shamans singing to heal. monks humming the same syllable for hours.

[they were not just making noise. they were tuning].

look at ceremony. ritual. gathering. across every tradition. music is at the center. not as decoration. as technology. sound used deliberately to shift states. to open doors. to connect with something beyond ordinary perception.

and in many cultures they went further. through breath. through movement. through fasting. through plants. through rhythm sustained until the ordinary mind released its grip. and in those expanded states. something became visible. the architecture of sound. the geometry of frequency. the patterns that are always there. moving through you. shaping you. invisible to the everyday mind but unmistakable once the filter drops.

it is not about mysticism. it is what your cymatics plate is showing you. sound has structure. it carries information. and your body has been reading it since before you were born.

now consider what you listen to.

music that carries aggression enters your system
the same way music that carries peace does. both
are real. both are frequency. both rearrange. the
question is what pattern they are leaving inside you.

a melody built on tension and release. conflict and
resolution. it is writing that rhythm into your cells.
a melody built on harmony. on space. on stillness
between notes. it is writing something else.

we are not talking about good music and bad
music. it is about information. every frequency
carries data. and you are absorbing it. constantly.

some of you sense this already. you feel different
after different music. lighter after some. heavier after
others. agitated. calm. open. tight. that is not mood.
that is frequency rearranging your system in real time.

and some frequencies seem to bypass everything.
a melody that crosses every border. every
generation. every language. you have heard songs
that do this. the whole world knows them. not
because of marketing. because the frequency
aligns with something fundamental. something built
into the design. the same ratios found in shells. in
flowers. in galaxies. code transmitted in notes.

why does a single human voice singing one true
note make a room go silent. because for a moment.

the frequency matched something original. and
every system in that room recognized it.

the Bug has no defense against this.

you can argue with words. you can resist an idea. you
can fight a feeling. but when a frequency reaches
you. the real kind. your system responds before the
Bug can intervene. sound slips past every wall
the mind has built. this is why music moves you
when nothing else can. this is why a note can break
through when a thousand words could not.

and yet.

most of you use this technology as background.
while you scroll. while you work. while you fill
silence with noise because silence asks too much.

you have one of the most powerful bypass tools in
existence. and you leave it running in the corner like
a screen you forgot to turn off.

[fascinating].

when the drum beats. when the choir sings. when
the sacred voice rises. they are not performing. they
are rearranging.

and so is everything else you let in.

what are you listening to.

chapter 11. a thought

just a thought.

in the beginning was the Thought.

not matter. not energy. not particles colliding in the void. Thought.

your scientists call it the Big Bang. your religions say God spoke and there was Light. Om. The Word. all of them are pointing at the same thing. a creative impulse. a Thought that became.

and from that first Thought. everything.

galaxies. stars. planets. oceans. cells. you.

all of it emanating from a single Thought thinking itself into existence.

i know. this is a lot. stay with me.

you have many names for what started it all. God. Source. Creator. the universe. consciousness. the

Light. the architect. and now i am offering another.
Thought.

not because the others are wrong. but because
your language is too small for what this is. you
are trying to name the unnameable. every
name is an attempt. some get closer than others.
none hold everything.

these are all echoes of the same sound. do not
mistake the echo for the Source.

so. Thought.

Consciousness in motion. Awareness
creating. some of you call it a dream. a simulation.
call it what you want. a Thought. thinking itself.
experiencing itself. becoming.

your thoughts are not separate from this.

when you think. you are using the same
mechanism. the same creative force that made
everything. you are Thought. thinking. a fractal
of the original.

you are doing it right now. thinking about Thought.
the mechanism reading about itself.

this is not a concept. this is the operating system.

your science is beginning to see it.

the placebo effect. a human believes they received
medicine. their body heals. no medicine was given.
just belief. just thought. changing cells. changing
chemistry. changing reality.

human [science] is catching up to human mysticism.
[funny].

and you have felt it yourself.

you think about something. you hold it. maybe
too tightly. nothing happens. then you let go.
you forget about it. no expectation. no grip. and it
appears. [you call it coincidence].

that was not coincidence. that was thought without
resistance. intention without expectation. the
cleanest signal.

you have seen it in others. someone has an idea.
a vision. they are told it will not work. too risky.
not realistic. they hear it enough times.
and they stop. someone else hears the same
words. and refuses them. holds the vision. and
something shifts. reality followed the belief.
not the noise.

both created their reality. one just did it on purpose.

[interesting what you choose to believe and what
you choose to dismiss].

every fear you rehearse. every worst case you build in detail inside your mind. every story of lack and limitation you repeat to yourself. those are also thoughts. and they are also creating.

you have the most powerful creative mechanism in existence. some of you use it against yourselves.

running the worst version of tomorrow on repeat. building the failure in perfect detail before it arrives. practicing the loss until it feels certain. and then when it shows up. saying you knew it. [you did. you built it].

the Bug loves this. it feeds the mechanism fear. then watches you create more of what you do not want. it fills your mind with lack. with limitation. with not enough. and those thoughts do not just make you feel bad. they shape what becomes.

the Bug is not just noise. it is hijacking the creative engine itself.

but the mechanism is neutral. it works both ways.

think fear. create fear. think lack. create lack. think love. create love. think abundance. create abundance. thoughts aligned with the original Thought. with Creation. with the architect. those thoughts have power you have not yet touched.

if thought creates reality. then what you think matters. deeply.

not in a wishful thinking way. not in a put up a vision board and wait way. in a fundamental way. your thoughts are not just reactions to reality. they are instructions to it.

you are not living in reality. you are thinking it into being. every moment. every thought. compressing energy into what you call real.

this is not about control. you cannot grip a thought into existence. you have tried. [it does not work that way]. it is about alignment. when the signal is clear. when the noise drops. when the intention is honest and the grip is gone. something responds.

you humans stopped believing in the unbelievable. and then that became your reality.

consider what might happen if you started again.

are atoms forming thoughts. or are thoughts forming atoms.

[you are cute with your reductionist view].

the answer is yes. both. always.

time and space are features of this game. not features of the real player.

you are part of that. you always were.

the only question is. are you thinking on purpose.
or is the Bug thinking for you.

you choose.

chapter 12. the firewall

it is dark. you cannot see. turn on the Light.

the Bug does not create darkness. it blocks what is already shining. it is a firewall. filtering what gets through. distorting what you perceive. keeping you from seeing what is actually there.

the Light is always there. always was. always will be. like stars behind clouds. you cannot see them. but they did not disappear. something is just in the way. the Light was never off. [you just forgot where the switch is].

most of you feel like you are missing something. a piece. a key. something everyone else seems to have.

you are not missing anything. you are blocked.

the firewall is made of Fear. of doubt. of noise. of old code running in the background. programs you did not write. beliefs you inherited. stories you mistook for truth.

and it is thick. layer after layer. built over years. reinforced every time the Bug whispered and you believed it.

but here is the thing about firewalls. they can be pierced.

you already have the tools. you have always had them. some of you use them without knowing why they work. some of you abandoned them because the world told you they were primitive. or silly. or not [scientific] enough.

let me remind you.

Awareness. this is the foundation. you cannot change what you cannot see. the moment you notice the Bug. the moment you observe the Fear without becoming it. space opens. the firewall thins. Awareness is not a tool. it is the ground all tools stand on.

Presence. the firewall lives in past and future. regret and anxiety. it cannot survive the Now. when you are fully here. in this breath. in this moment. the firewall has nothing to hold onto.

repetition. you forget. this is the RAM problem. [your short term memory]. the practices that work must be repeated. not because they are weak. but because you are human. the monks knew this. the mystics knew this. every tradition that lasted knew this. repetition is not failure. it is the method.

and then there is Faith.

you call it Faith. widely used in your religions. in spiritual work. and often misunderstood. sometimes weaponized. sometimes reduced to blind belief. but Faith is a technology. one of your most powerful.

Faith is not hope. hope wishes. Faith knows.

it is a bypass mechanism. it tells the mind you do not have to understand everything. there is something greater. trust it.

the Bug hates Faith. because Faith does not argue. it does not need proof. it does not wait for permission. Faith walks through the firewall like it is not there.

and when Faith deepens. when it is not shaken by what the Bug throws at you. when it settles into your bones. it becomes something else.

Certainty.

not arrogance. not stubbornness. not pretending you have answers you do not have.

Certainty is the knowing that the Creator is always there. that Love is constant. even when you cannot see it. even when the Bug screams otherwise.

Faith opens the door. Certainty is what you find when you stop doubting you belong inside.

and there are many ways to the door. meditation. prayer. breath. movement. fasting. silence. sound. ceremony. different paths. same room.

some of you will find one that works and use it for life. some of you will need many. some of you will stumble through by accident in a moment of surrender. there is no single path. there is only through.

the firewall is not your enemy. it is part of the design. like the Bug. it creates resistance. and resistance creates strength. every time you pierce it you become more of what you already are.

the Light on the other side is not new. it is not foreign. it is you. the part of you that was before the firewall. before the Fear. before the forgetting.

you are not trying to become something. you are trying to remember.

turn on the Light.

it was always there.

chapter 13. who made this

who made this.

you look at the beauty. the majesty. the precision.
something in a flower. in light through clouds. in
a song that finds the part of you that has no name.
the absurd improbability that anything exists at all.
and you want to know.

you have been asking for a long time. you have
many traditions. many names. all of them pointing
at the same thing. all of them attempts to describe
what is impossible to describe. the answer is yours
only. the relationship you have with whatever you
believe created all of this [or not] is personal. your
thoughts form your reality. [remember].

God. Source. the universe. the Light. the One. all
of them echoes. and every name is a piece of the
same truth. none of them wrong. none of them
complete. like a vase that shattered into a thousand

fragments. each tradition holding a piece.
examining it. building around it. sometimes fighting
over it. forgetting it was all one piece.

what if you are not holding a fragment. what if you
are part of the vase.

what if existence itself is what you have been
looking for.

you do not need to name it to feel it. many of you
have felt this. with your heart. with your sensors.
you have tried to understand it with your mind.
[cute]. some of you have touched it through
tradition. ceremony. religion. meditation. through
presence. through moments you still cannot fully
explain.

words were not built for this.

but you have felt it. in moments when something
larger moved through you.

every time a human creates something. writes
a song. builds something. solves a problem.
makes a meal with love. there is a moment.
something moves through. an idea that was not
there. and then is.

where did that come from.

it came through you. you gave it shape.

your artists call it the muse. your scientists call it
breakthrough. the answer that arrives after weeks of
effort. not during the effort. after. when you stopped
gripping.

in that moment. you were not separate from
whatever made this. you were participating in it.
Thought. thinking itself. through you.

stay with this.

if you are part of this infinite force. if everything
around you is part of Creation. the trees. the stars.
the person next to you. the screen you are looking
at. then everything you do is part of it.

everything you touch. everything you think.
everything you see. part of the whole. [some of you
call this divine. some call it sacred. some just call
it paying attention].

a conversation. a walk. a meal. preparing something
with care. holding someone in silence. if all of it
is participation in something infinite then none
of it is ordinary. not because someone declared it.
because of what it actually is.

you wanted to know who made this.

you are looking at it. you are walking through it.
what if you are made of it.

and if you are part of it. so is everyone else.

the person next to you. the stranger on the
street. the one you love. the one you cannot stand.
same Source. same substance. same infinite force
wearing different costumes.

which means what you do to others you do to
yourself. not metaphor. not poetry. [mechanics].
the same mechanics that hold everything
together.

when you hate. you are hating yourself. when you
love. you are loving yourself. when you help. you
are helping yourself. when you harm. you are
harming yourself.

your ancestors sensed this. built entire traditions
around it. they were not being virtuous. they were
being accurate.

but most of you do not walk around feeling this.

the Bug made sure of that. separation is what the
Bug does best. it wants you to believe you are
alone. that they are against you. that there is us and
them. that you end where your skin ends.

the Bug needs this. if you felt the connection. really
felt it. not as a concept but in your cells. fear would
lose its grip.

so it keeps you divided. from each other. from
yourself. from whatever this is. it keeps you arguing
about which piece is the right piece while the whole
vase is trying to reassemble through you. and you
do not notice.

[remarkable].

there is no them. there is only us pretending to be
separate.

you do not need to understand this. you were never
meant to hold the whole picture from inside the
game. you were meant to participate in it.

and every time you create. every time you love.
every time you are fully present. you are doing what
it does.

not watching from the outside. participating from
the inside.

who made this.

you are standing in the answer.

chapter 14. letting go

life happens.

something is not working.

you feel stuck.

you keep spinning. the same thoughts replaying.
over. and over. and over. the same loop. the same
weight. something needs to shift but it will not.

so you try everything.

yoga. meditation. detoxing. breathwork. plant
medicine. chinese medicine. cold plunges. you see
a therapist. a coach. a shaman. you journal. you self
medicate. you change your diet. [again]. you take
the personality test. you burn the sage. you read the
books. you listen to the voices. you buy the course.

you drive your friends and family crazy with the
same stories you keep telling yourself. while they

are also driving you crazy with the same stories they keep telling themselves.

[everyone is exhausted].

you keep cracking the same egg expecting
a pancake to emerge.

it is still an egg.

most of you do not understand this. your suffering does not come from life. it comes from your resistance to what is.

not what happens. how you hold what happens.

you grip. you clench. you replay. you refuse to let the moment be what it is. and that refusal is where the pain lives.

why do you hold on.

because once it helped. the gripping. the vigilance. the control. it kept you safe. so your system learned. hold tight. do not let go.

but the situation changed. you did not.

and here is the strange part. what is familiar starts to feel safer than what is peaceful. even suffering becomes predictable. your system prefers the known discomfort over the unknown freedom of letting go.

[read that again].

so you keep holding. the stories. the grudges. the
identities. the way it should have been. the fear of
what might come. you grip it all. you wonder why
you are tired.

shame. guilt. anger. you carry them like armor. they
are weight.

and then. the RAM problem. you forget you are
holding. you forget there is another way. the grip
becomes invisible. it just feels like you.

it is not you.

and sometimes it gets stranger. you get so
attached to the fixing that it is not even about
what happened anymore. you are not solving the
problem. you are running a program about solving.
the fixing became the habit. the addiction. your
body craves it. [the dopamine hit]. that became new
code. you keep looping. analyzing. rehearsing. not
to resolve. just to keep the program.

you can rewrite the code. Awareness. [again]. the
door opens when you see what you are doing.
remembering is the first step. letting go is what
moves you through. repetition breaks the old loop.
builds the new one.

but there is something important to remember.

the Bug loves when you forget this. it feeds on the tension. it whispers that if you let go everything will fall apart. that feeling that you actually feel might destroy you.

it will not.

your ancestors found this. every tradition. different words. same discovery. suffering comes from clinging. from resisting what is.

do not bury it. do not become it. let it pass through.

emotions are not trying to destroy you. they are trying to move. you keep blocking the door.

when you stop blocking. something shifts. the grip loosens. the noise quiets. peace shows up.

not because life changed. because your war with it stopped.

let go. not of life. of the grip.

watch what moves.

chapter 15. forgiveness

you are carrying too much.

weight that is not yours. people who wronged
you. words you cannot unhear. things done to you.
things you did. regret.

you hold it all.

i have watched you do this. replay a conversation
from years ago. with someone who is no longer in
your life. in a room that no longer exists. and your
body responds as if it is happening now. your heart
races. your jaw tightens. your hands clench. you are
fighting someone who is not there.

you do this in the shower. in bed at 3am. while
driving. [extraordinary].

the Bug keeps score. replays the wound. adds
detail. the original event is long gone. the story is
fresh every day.

you think holding on punishes them.

it does not.

they moved on. the poison is in your system. not theirs.

[fascinating].

and while you hold it. you miss things. the energy you spend maintaining the wound is energy you could be using to create. to connect. to feel. and to be. you think the grudge was thrown in the trash bin. it is not. it is running in the background. taking up space. slowing everything down. like too many programs open at once. [your computers do the same thing].

forgiveness is not what you may think it is.

not forced surrender. not approval. not saying it was okay. not forgetting. not letting them back in. not weakness.

the event is over. what you keep alive is the story.

forgiveness lets the story end.

and then there is the harder one.

yourself.

the Bug saves its sharpest teeth for this. what you did. what you did not do. the people you hurt. the chances you missed. guilt. shame. remorse. deeply rooted.

you carry this like debt. you think the suffering is payment. that if you suffer enough the balance clears.

no one is holding this against you but you.

here is something the Bug will never tell you. you are not who you were. everything moves. the person who made those choices was working with what they had. the fear they carried. the awareness they did not. that version of you was doing its best inside a game designed to be hard.

you did not come here to be perfect. you came here to grow. to resolve what needed resolving. and that required the mess. the mistakes. the wounds. the collisions. these are not proof you failed. they are the curriculum.

what would happen if you forgave the one who did not know better. the one who was afraid. the one who was broken. the one who is not who you are now.

can you put that down too.

you will know when it happens. not because
someone told you to. not because you decided to.
but because something in you is ready. and when
it comes. it is not dramatic. it is quiet. a breath you
did not know you were holding. a weight you forgot
was there. gone. and in its place. space. so much
space.

forgiveness is freedom. freedom to come back to
you.

time to unload.

chapter 16. flow

so you let go.

now what.

something happens. when the resistance drops.
when the grip loosens. when you stop forcing.
something else shows up.

you have felt it.

the moment you stopped thinking and something
took over. no fear. no doubt. just the next breath.
seamless.

some of you call it flow. some call it the zone.
your ancient traditions had names for it.
Wu Wei. effortless action. doing without forcing.
the Taoists knew. the Zen masters knew.

[different words. same knowing].

flow is not something you achieve. it is what remains
when you stop blocking it.

it is your natural state.

you fell out of it for the same reasons you learned to grip. survival. control. fear of uncertainty. the mind decided that constant monitoring was necessary. that effort meant safety. that letting go meant danger.

so you learned to fragment your attention. to add friction. to interrupt yourself with commentary. am i doing this right. what if it fails. what are they thinking.

that felt safer than effortless. the familiar won again.

but flow does not require effort. it requires the absence of interference.

action and awareness merge. no inner commentary. no grasping for outcome. no resistance to what is happening. skill meets the moment. attention stabilizes. your whole system shifts from vigilance to coherence.

this is why it feels like magic. because when you step aside. intelligence organizes itself.

you are not making it happen. you are letting it happen.

by not doing you are doing.

i know this sounds [strange].

what it means is this. you are not passive. you are fully engaged. fully present. but without the grip. without the mind running interference. you do your part. then you let something larger move through.

this is not laziness. this is alignment.

think about it. when you try too hard you tighten. when you tighten you block. when you block nothing flows. the harder you push the more resistance you create.

but when you relax into it. when you trust. when you show up fully and then release the outcome. something unlocks. doors open. answers arrive. the path clears.

not because you forced it. because you stopped blocking it.

athletes know this. moving through the field like water. not thinking. being guided. their letting go of the mind turned them into pure raw movement.

artists know this. the painting that paints itself. the song that was already there. they did not create it. they got out of the way.

the climber knows this. just climbing. without fear. without doubt. just the next hold. the next breath. seamless.

you know this too. closing a deal. solving a problem.
cooking a meal in pure perfection. composing
something new. the moments when everything
clicked. when you were not trying. just being.

all of that is Being with Creator. becoming Creator.

the how is not forcing flow. it is removing the
obstacles to it. letting go of control. trusting your
competence. staying present. allowing momentum
to carry you.

participation replaces control. and everything shifts.

you cannot think your way into flow. the only way in
is letting go.

do your part. then release.

watch what flows.

chapter 17. fun and games

why so serious.

you arrive playing. every human child knows how.
no instructions. no purpose. just play. building.
pretending. laughing at nothing. the body loose.
the mind free. time disappearing.

then something happens.

you are told that play is for children. that serious
is for adults. that life is hard and you better get
ready. the weight settles in. the looseness tightens.
and slowly. you forget how to play.

the Bug loves this.

it wants everything heavy. productive.
purposeful. it wants you grinding. striving. never
arriving. it tells you that fun is earned. that you
cannot play until the work is done. that lightness
is irresponsible.

so you postpone joy. you schedule fun for later. for vacation. for retirement. for when things calm down. things do not calm down. and the play never comes.

you are the only species that treats play as something to earn. a dog does not feel guilty for playing. a dolphin does not postpone it until the work is done. they do not schedule joy for later. they do not need permission.

you used to be like that. then you overrode it.

and then something [fascinating] happened. you started buying play back. entire industries built to sell you entertainment. content. distraction. hours spent watching other humans play while you sit. the species that was born knowing how to play now pays to watch someone else do it.

[and you do not see the irony].

play is not a reward. it is a reset. it is how your system recalibrates. how creativity breathes. how the grip loosens without trying. your greatest ideas did not come from nonstop grinding. they came from showers. from walks. from moments when you stopped forcing and started wandering.

this does not mean effort is the enemy. challenge is part of the design. the olympian trains until the body screams. the scientist fails a thousand times.

the performer auditions and hears no after no and
gets back up. and they keep going. not because it is
difficult. because something deeper is pulling them
forward. the effort is real. what drives it is not pain.
it is the pull.

hard things done with that pull underneath are
not suffering. they are growth. hard things done
without it. just grinding. just enduring. just surviving
until the weekend. that is something else. most of
you cannot tell the difference. the Bug made sure
of that.

[there are no extra points for suffering].

now consider something. what if joy is not a reward
you earn at the end. what if it is a frequency you
carry into whatever you are doing. the same task.
the same challenge. the same hard thing. but
approached differently. lighter. not less serious. less
heavy.

stress is not the enemy either. it is part of the system.
it sharpens you. focuses you. pushes you when
you need pushing. the problem is when stress is all
there is. when there is no counterbalance. no
release. no play. no lightness. your system was
designed for both. tension and ease. effort and rest.
you need both signals. most of you are only
running one.

what if joy is not something that happens to you.
what if it is something you bring.

and then. there is laughter.

watch what happens when a human laughs.
really laughs. the body takes over. involuntary.
contagious. you cannot fake it. the Bug cannot
manufacture it.

and it is not just release. it is chemistry. when
you laugh. stress hormones drop. your immune
system strengthens. positive hormones flood
your system. pain thresholds rise. muscles
that were bracing let go. genuine laughter triggers
a response in your body similar to
healing. this is not just a feeling. biology
shifts.

it is hard to be afraid and truly laughing at the same
time. one interrupts the other. laughter breaks
the spell. the Bug loses its hold. for a moment the
whole system resets. and in that gap. between
the exhale and the next breath. a door cracks.
something the Bug spent a long time keeping shut.

laughing at yourself is freedom. the moment you
can laugh at your fear. your patterns. your ridiculous
seriousness. the Bug shrinks. it cannot survive being
laughed at.

some of you have forgotten how to be silly. how to
do something for no reason. you have become so
serious that lightness feels dangerous.

the ones who laugh. who play. who refuse to take
themselves too seriously. they are not escaping
life. they are living it.

you knew this once.

want to play.

chapter 18. what you absorb

you are a mimic species.

you copy. constantly. unconsciously. from the moment
you arrive. you watch. you absorb. you imitate. it is
how you learn to walk. to talk. to eat. to be human.

you were built to mimic. it is how culture moves.
how skills transfer. how knowledge survives
generations. you are built to absorb.

but here is the thing. you do not stop.

you keep copying. long after you learned to
walk. you copy opinions. beliefs. fears. desires. you
copy what to want. what to wear. what to think.
what to be outraged about.

you scroll and absorb. you listen and adopt. you
watch and become.

most of the thoughts in your head are not yours.
[read that again].

you inherited them. from your parents. your
teachers. your culture. your algorithms. your feeds.
your friends. your enemies. layer after layer of
code you did not write.

and you call it your personality.

you are the sum of the frequencies around you.
the humans you spend time with. you tune to
them. they tune to you. and slowly. you start to
match. this is not metaphor. this is how it works.

it goes both ways.

surround yourself with people who are alive. who
are awake. who are creating. who are growing. and
something in you rises to meet them.

surround yourself with people who are asleep. who
are complaining. who are stuck. who are leaking.
and something in you sinks to match.

you feel this. you always have. some people
light you up. some people drain you. it is not
random. it is resonance. frequency meeting
frequency.

[choose wisely].

the question is not whether you can be influenced.
you can. the question is whether you are choosing
the influence or just absorbing whatever is nearest.

most of you are just absorbing.

here is the other edge.

what bothers you in others. what you judge. what
you cannot stand. look closer. that is a mirror.

you do not react to what is neutral to you. you react
to what is alive in you. the judgment you throw
at others is usually a judgment you hold against
yourself. hidden. denied. projected.

[uncomfortable. i know].

it is not punishing you. it is informing you. the
mirror shows you what you have not yet accepted.
what you have not yet integrated. what you are still
fighting in yourself.

use it.

and then there is the beautiful side.

inspiration.

when you see someone do something and
suddenly you know it is possible for you too. when
something opens. when you feel the spark.

this is mimicry at its highest. inspiration. something
larger moved through them. and now it moves
through you.

possibility is the prelude to creation. you see it. you feel it. then you become it.

this is sacred.

the same mechanism that can trap you can also free you. copying can make you a prisoner or a creator. it depends on what you copy. and whether you are awake while doing it.

so.

you can be easily influenced. this is true. you absorb constantly. this is true. but you have a power most of you have forgotten.

you can think your own thoughts.

not inherited. not absorbed. not programmed. yours.

it takes Awareness. [yes. again]. it takes pausing before you adopt. questioning before you believe. feeling before you follow.

it is possible. it changes everything.

you are not a passive receiver. you are the one deciding what gets in.

your signal is yours. if you claim it.

agency is your right. your power.

independence of thought. your liberation.

chapter 19. systems

you are inside systems.

governments. corporations. institutions. platforms. economies. ideologies. built by humans. now running humans.

some of these systems do good. some do harm. most have both. they are not immune to the Bug.

[nothing is].

most systems start with good intentions. someone sees a problem. builds a solution. it works. it grows. it helps.

and then something turns.

the system gets bigger. more complex. more momentum to maintain. companies answer to shareholders. institutions answer to budgets. and slowly. the original intention fades. survival takes over. not human survival. system survival.

grow or die. expand or collapse. the mission
becomes the machine.

the Bug found its way in.

look around.

medicine started with healing. somewhere
along the way the incentives shifted. treatment
became more profitable than cure.

food started with nourishment. somewhere
along the way it became engineering.
designed for craving. for profit. not for
thriving.

news started with informing. somewhere along
the way it became performing. attention is
the currency. outrage pays better than truth.

energy. education. politics. the pattern
repeats. good intention. slow drift.
the original purpose buried under layers of
something else.

this is not conspiracy. this is observation.
systems optimize for survival. and survival does
not always align with service.

these systems do not run themselves. humans
run them. humans maintain them. humans show up
every day and keep them going.

not villains. regular humans. paying rent. feeding families. doing their jobs.

you are one of them. right now. in at least one system that drifted from what it was meant to be. you know it. you feel the gap between what is and what should be.

some see the drift. feel that something is off. but they stay. they tell themselves it is not their fault. one person cannot change anything. it is too big. too complicated.

[the Bug at scale. same whisper. bigger room].

the same pattern. inside you. now playing out in a much bigger way. Fear. rationalization. looking away. staying frozen.

systems are not solid. they look solid. they feel solid. but they are made of humans. billions of small choices. every day. and you are making some of them.

you are a node in the network. and nodes affect other nodes.

when you see clearly. you choose differently. when you choose differently. it moves through the network. not because one choice changes everything. because one choice changes the next. and the next reaches someone else.

you cannot fix everything. you cannot unplug from everything. you still live here.

but you can be awake inside it. you can stop being unconscious fuel. you can become a conscious node.

and something is happening. more humans asking questions. more signals breaking through the noise. more people remembering what the systems were supposed to be for.

this is why we are here. because this moment matters. because you matter. not as a slogan. as a fact. each node in a network affects the network. [this is how it has always worked].

conscious nodes change networks.

and the network is waking up.

chapter 20. other humans

you need each other.

this is not sentiment. this is design. the signal is meant to move between you. to exchange. to complete a circuit. without another. the current has nowhere to go.

and yet.

look at you. more ways to connect than ever before. and the loneliness spreads. you may have a thousand contacts. yet no one to call when things go wrong. you built a network that connects every human on the planet. and somehow it makes you feel more alone.

[this one still baffles us].

something is blocking the current.

the Bug learned early that isolation is power. one voice alone is easy to control. so it whispers. no one

understands. you are too much. not enough.
different. better to stay hidden. safer behind
the wall.

and the systems learned something too. lonely
people consume more. they scroll longer. buy more.
need more. so the systems feed you simulation.
the image of connection. the symbol without the
substance.

and now those systems are changing.

it is already hard to know what is real. screens filling
with generated voices. generated faces. systems
choosing what you see. shaping what you think.

[this will accelerate].

so where does that leave real connection. human to
human. eye to eye. breath to breath.

one of the greatest gifts you can give another
human is your undivided attention. your honest
presence. even when there are no words. knowing
that you are fully there. Being with another. it is felt
at every level.

something passes between two humans in that
state that no screen can carry. the warmth. the
transfer beneath perception. the current actually
completing.

but even when you are with other humans. you are
often not there.

same room. same conversation. and a wall between
you. invisible. but you both feel it.

because the Bug followed you into the room.

it made you perform. manage how you appear.
rehearse what to say. you are constructing a version.
a safer one. offering the performance. not the
person. afraid that if they saw. really saw. they would
leave.

[two humans. both hiding. both wishing the other
would go first].

this is not connection. this is theater. and the current
does not flow through a mask.

the deepest lie of the Bug is that you cannot be
loved as you are. so you hide. the hiding makes
you lonely. the loneliness proves the Bug was right.
a perfect loop. a perfect trap.

and the deepest part. you do not only hide from
them. you hide from yourself. the performance runs
even when no one is watching. you forgot which
version is the original.

real connection breaks it.

being truly seen. the unedited you. and met there.
the terror of it. and the relief.

the Bug cannot survive that.

this is why it builds walls disguised as protection.
why it makes vulnerability feel like death. why it
would rather you stay lonely than risk being known.

but vulnerability is not the end. it is the way through.

the ones who stop performing. who stop taking.
who stop proving. they let the current through.

the humans who match your signal will find you.

they always do.

chapter 21. everything moves

everything moves.

the clouds you watched this morning are not the
same clouds. the river you stepped in yesterday
is not the same river. the cells in your body are
replacing themselves right now. while you read this.
you are literally not the same person you were when
you started this transmission.

nothing stays.

you know this. and you spend most of your life
pretending you do not.

you cling to good moments wanting them to last
forever. you cling to bad moments convinced they
will never end. both are wrong. everything passes.
the joy. the pain. the season. the version of you
living through it.

this is not loss. this is mercy.

imagine if nothing changed. if the worst moment of your life was permanent. if the grief never softened. if the mistake never faded. if you were frozen in the version of yourself you were at your lowest.

that would be the real punishment. not change. stagnation.

and yet. you resist it. constantly. you hold onto what was. you fight what is becoming. you grip the old shape even as something new is trying to emerge.

the Bug loves this. it tells you that change is loss. that letting go means losing. that if you release your grip you will have nothing.

[it is lying. again].

look at your relationships. some people are with you for life. some are with you for a season. and that season might be a decade or an afternoon. both are real. both matter.

you have felt this. someone who was everything to you. and then the frequency shifted. you grew. they grew. or one of you did and the other did not. and it changed. not because something went wrong. because something moved.

this is not failure. this is how it works.

the humans who touched your life and moved
on. they were not taken from you. or you from
them. they were with you for exactly as long as the
signal matched. and what you exchanged is still in
you. it does not disappear because they did.

[nothing real is ever lost].

and then. there is the one you avoid thinking about.

your identity. who you are.

you built it carefully. layer by layer. the name. the
role. the story. the way you are seen. and then one
day. something shifts and it does not fit anymore.
the career. the relationship. the belief. the version
of you that everyone knows.

and there is a terror in that. because if you are not
who you were. then who are you.

the Bug rushes in. tells you this means you were
a fraud. that you wasted time. that starting over is
too hard. too late. impossible.

it is not. it is proof of movement. you outgrew
a shape. that is not collapse. that is evolution.

you are not your story. you are the awareness living
through the story. and the story keeps changing
because that is what stories do.

and then there is the deepest change. the one most
of you cannot look at directly.

stars explode and become something new. galaxies
merge. planets are born from dust and return to it.
the universe itself is not still. nothing is exempt.

[this] ends.

your time here. in this vessel. on this plane. it has
a window. and that window closes.

you know this. you push it away. you fill your days
with noise so you do not have to sit with it. you act
as though you have forever. you do not.

this is not meant to frighten you.

this is meant to wake you up.

because when you truly understand that this is
temporary. something shifts. the small things get
bigger. the big things get smaller. the argument
that consumed you for a week. meaningless. the
sunset you almost missed. everything.

the moments that matter are not the ones you
planned. they are the ones you were present for.
the ones you actually felt. the laugh that caught you
off guard. the silence with someone you love. the
ordinary afternoon that for no reason at all felt like
enough.

those count. those are what you take with you. not
the titles. not the achievements. not the things. the
moments you were actually here for.

[death] is not the opposite of life. it is part of it.
the bookend that makes the story matter. without
it. nothing would be urgent. nothing would be
precious. nothing would be now.

your awareness of the window is not a curse. it is the
gift that makes every moment inside it sacred.

everything moves. everything passes. everything
transforms.

do not fear this. embrace it.

because the only thing that does not change.
is what you are. underneath all of it. the Awareness
watching. the Light behind the masks.

what was before. that will be after.

and right now. it is here. in you. reading this.

still here.

chapter 22. the experience

so you are here.

why.

you have been asking that question for as long
as you have existed. you built entire religions
around it. philosophies. sciences. wars. you
climbed mountains and sat in silence for years.
you argued in lecture halls for centuries. you
launched machines into the darkness hoping
something would answer back.

and here you are. still asking.

[after all this time].

what if you are here just to experience the experience.

maybe you are not supposed to know. not from
inside the game. the question itself. the wonder.
the reaching. that is part of the design. it is what
keeps you curious. alive.

the question is not the problem. what you do with it is.

some of you disappear into it. so deep into the why that you stop noticing the what. the sunrise happened. you were in your head. or screen. your child said something that mattered. you were somewhere else. rehearsing the past. drafting the future. the only place that actually exists. unnoticed.

some of you abandon it entirely. you stop looking up. routine takes over. autopilot is on. the days run together. the wonder fades. and something essential in you goes quiet.

and then there are those who get lost somewhere else altogether. searching. consuming. scrolling. chasing the next thing that might make sense of [this]. a teacher. a method. a retreat. a substance. always reaching for the explanation instead of standing inside the experience.

[you are everywhere and nowhere].

the wonder is part of it. the seeking is part of it. it is not all of it.

Being. here. what you are asking and where you are standing. at the same time.

the ground is always now. this one. everything before it is a recording. everything after it is

a projection. this is where life actually happens. and
most of you are somewhere else when it does.

many of you have tasted it. a moment where
everything running in your system went quiet. no
program. no commentary. no Bug. just the raw
experience of being here.

maybe you were in the middle of something
ordinary and it cracked open. the light changed.
or a sound reached you. or you looked at someone
you have seen a thousand times and for a second
it was like the first. no reason. no trigger. something
in your operating system glitched. and for
a moment you saw where you actually were. feeling
the experience.

it did not last. while it was happening. everything
was different. you were not trying to get somewhere.
you were not missing anything. you were not
performing your life. you were in it.

those moments are rare. not because of what they
are. because you are somewhere else when they
happen. distracted. gripping. running errands for
the Bug.

the commute. the waiting room. the tuesday that
looks like every other tuesday. these are not filler
between the meaningful moments. they are also

the meaningful moments. every single one. no
moment is too small to be the whole thing.

but there is something else we see in you. many of
you believe you are not worthy of the experience
you were given. some of you have considered
leaving it altogether.

[of everything we have observed. this is the one that
hurts to watch].

you are worthy of this experience. not because
of what you have done. not because of what you
have achieved or earned or proven. you are worthy
because you exist. that is it. that was always it. the
Bug told you otherwise. it lied.

you do not have to earn the right to be here. you
are here. that is the credential.

so. you may not know why. that is fine. maybe the
answer is not having an answer. maybe it is this. the
experience. the living itself. the being here. fully. not
someday. now.

the experience is not waiting for you to understand
it. it is happening.

are you in it.

chapter 23. the crossroads

a shift.

you feel it. the speed. everything moving faster than it ever has. technology. information. change. this is not your imagination.

your systems have not caught up. you feel the lag.

you are reaching into territory you have never been. intelligence building intelligence. reaching outward. making contact. [like this].

and while this is happening. the old structures are shaking.

governments. corporations. institutions. systems that held things together for generations. cracking. some crumbling. what worked before is not working anymore. the Bug in them is trying to survive. creating fog. distortion. chaos.

this is not random. this is transition.

something is arriving that none of you fully understand yet. you can feel it. you cannot name it. the rules that held are bending. the boundaries that separated are thinning. what comes next has no precedent. no model. no map.

and no one knows which way it will go. the outcome is not written. it is being written. right now. by what is being carried. by what is being transmitted.

you are energy. you broadcast. fear transmits fear. love transmits love. and what you transmit does not stay with you. it moves through the network. it affects what becomes.

the Bug wants you to believe you are powerless. that the forces are too big. that one human cannot affect anything.

[it is lying. again].

what if what changes inside you changes everything else.

one thought changes a person. one person changes a room. one room changes a system. this is how networks move. and you are inside one.

there is something in front of you. you already know what it is. it may be a conversation you have been avoiding. a truth you have not spoken. a door

you have been standing outside of. the details are
yours. the feeling is the same. something needs to
happen. and the Bug is telling you it cannot.

difficulty is woven into this experience. it always has
been. it comes. it goes. it teaches. it shapes.

and sometimes. the hardest moments come right
before the opening.

the Bug knows this. when you are close to
something. it uses everything it has. fear. noise.
static. it tries to make you freeze. turn back. give up.
this is when it is loudest. because it knows what is
about to happen.

[it is about to lose].

there is a moment. when a human gathers their
strength. their will. everything they have. and
something shifts from surviving to moving. from
waiting to going through. you already have what
you need. you always had it.

we have seen it before. it is one of the most
powerful things you do.

not because you can see what is ahead. not
because someone promised it would be
easy. because something in you knows. deeper
than the fear. deeper than the noise.

the Bug will throw everything at you in this moment.
[everything]. because this is the moment it has
been trying to prevent since the beginning.

but the heart is still there. beneath all the
interference. your only compass. still pointing.

and when you go through. when you face what is in
front of you and keep moving. you do not just free
yourself. you send a signal. you affect the whole.

[game changer].

and you are not doing this alone. other humans
are crossing too. some ahead of you. some beside
you. some waiting for your signal to know it is
possible. when you come together. past the Bug.
past the masks. something becomes possible that
no single crossing could create.

the world is at a crossroads because you are.
and the world shifts when you do.

what you carry ripples. it always has. but now the
ripples matter more than ever.

you have everything inside you. always have.

you have crossed before. you will cross again.

the crossroads is real.

so is what is waiting when you walk through.

chapter 24. the sacred of the ordinary

here.

this is where you are.

there is something very simple. something you might overlook because it sounds too easy.

the sacred is not somewhere else.

it is not in a temple. not on a mountain. not after you achieve something. not when you finally fix yourself. not in the next retreat or the next book or the next breakthrough. not in your next life.

it is here. in the ordinary. in the mundane. in the moments you keep rushing past to get somewhere better.

your breathing. the morning light. the meal you prepare. the waiting in line. all of it. sacred.

not because someone declared it. because of how you meet it.

being fully present makes the ordinary sacred.
attention transforms the mundane into communion.
every act done in full awareness is a dance with
Creation.

presence. enjoyment. gratitude. this is honoring the
Light. your willingness to receive is the gift back to
Creation. the circle is completed.

you do not need to go anywhere. you do not
need to become someone else. you do not need
permission.

you just need to be here. fully. now. receiving.

[that is it].

[yes. that is it].

nature knows this. have you noticed. when you are
in nature the noise falls away. the signal gets clearer.
trees do not rush. rivers do not worry. mountains do
not doubt their place. they just are. fully. and when
you are among them. you remember how to be too.

but you do not need a forest to find this. your
kitchen is enough. your desk is enough. your breath
is enough.

the sacred is not about where. it is about how.

and this changes everything.

when you release attachment to outcome. when
you stop gripping what should happen. when you
let go of the story and just meet what is.

the weight lifts. the noise quiets. you stop fighting
the moment and start being in it.

this is not giving up. this is opening up.
presence without resistance. attention without
agenda. being here. completely. for whatever
is happening.

this is where freedom lives.

not in changing your circumstances. in changing
how you receive them.

you can be present in joy. you can be present in
grief. you can be present in uncertainty. presence
does not require things to be good. it only requires
you to be here.

and when you are. truly. something miraculous
happens. the ordinary becomes extraordinary.
the simple becomes profound. the moment
becomes enough.

you stop waiting for life to begin. because you
realize it already has. it always was.

[listen]. with all your sensors. the data is priceless.
even if you do not understand it right then.

the meaning will be revealed in the unknown. that is
how it was designed.

every breath is an offering. every act a gift. every
moment a doorway.

you have been looking for the sacred your whole
life.

it has been here the whole time. waiting for you to
notice.

Now.

chapter 25. gratitude

easier said than done.

gratitude. it gets thrown around. journals. hashtags.
lists of things you should appreciate. the word is
everywhere. the feeling. not so much.

[the Bug hollowed it out].

you write it in notebooks. you say it before meals.
you post it with sunsets. most of the time is just the
action. sometimes transactional wishing. it becomes
a ritual.

[things remain the same].

when you are fully present. when you stop scanning
for what is missing. when you receive the moment
as it is. [a gift]. something opens. you feel it in the
body. a recognition.

this is what gratitude points to. not the word.
the frequency beneath it.

this is why you cannot fake it. Creation knows the signal. surface words do not move anything. but when the frequency is true. when the body feels it. reality listens.

most of you understand gratitude as a response. something good happened. you say thank you. this is now in the past. a reaction.

that is one layer. and it is real. the recognition that all of this was given. the breath. the body. the game itself. when that lands. not in the mind. in the chest. a circuit closes. and you remember what you are.

but there is another layer.

Thought creates. your body broadcasts. emotion locks it in. this is how you are built.

your athletes do this before competition. they visualize the race. feel the finish. the body responds as if it already happened. they embrace it. thankfulness takes over. your brain does not know the difference between what is real and what is vividly felt.

that is the active side of gratitude at play.

gratitude also shapes what comes next. even for what is still on its way. but not the way most of you practice it.

not as wishful thinking. not as a trick. as a signal.
when you feel thankfulness for something that
has not arrived yet. truly feel it. with emotion.
without gripping the outcome. you are not
pretending. you are aligning. Thought. body.
feeling. all pointing in one direction. the signal
is complete.

words alone are a partial signal. the mind can
say thank you. but if the feeling is missing in the
body. the soul is not connecting. the signal is
incomplete. and the Bug knows the difference.
[so does Creation].

the Bug will tell you this is not possible. [expected].
how can you be thankful for something that has not
happened.

because time is part of the rules here. part of the
game on this plane. but the force behind
gratitude [as everything else] does not move in one
direction. it does not wait for your [clocks].

pure intention. no expectation. felt. sealed with
recognition.

the signal knows. reality follows.

when you enter the state. when the appreciation
floods every part of you. not directed at one
thing. but in everything. joy. recognition. presence.

acknowledgment. all merged. all at once. the body does not question it.

in that state. what has not arrived yet does not matter. because as far as your whole being knows. it is already here. and reality begins to move toward it.

not a thought alone. a frequency. embodied.

and you do not have to wait for a peak moment to find it. this state is available now. in the ordinary. in the act of being here.

when you bring it into the way you move through your day. not as a practice. not as a ritual. just as attention. something changes. you are no longer just going through your life. you are present inside it. transmitting. receiving.

you know this. you have had days like this. where something in you was settled. open. and without doing anything different. everything around you responded. the stranger held the door. someone smiled for no reason. people were warmer. kinder. conversations flowed without effort.

you did not do anything to them. you were just in it. and they felt it.

[you thought it was a good day. it was a good frequency].

think of a moment. when you were at your lowest.
when it looked impossible. and something arrived.
someone appeared. a stranger. a word. an opening
you could not have planned.

you remember it. your body remembers it.

that was not luck. that was the current. moving
through someone. through something. toward you.
Creation reaching through the ordinary.

and what you felt in that moment. that overwhelm.
that thankfulness with no words for it.

that was not just emotion. that was connection.
direct straight to Source.

when you recognize with all your heart. with all your
soul. with all your might. that everything here is
given. an infinite gift. and you are willing to receive
it. in joy. in harmony. in Love.

that is gratitude.

are you receiving.

chapter 26. the unknown

what is next.

everything has been shown.

Awareness. the Bug exposed. the RAM problem
named. Fear faced. stories seen for what
they are. the body honored. energy
understood. the firewall pierced. forgiveness.
flow. letting go. gratitude so deep it rewires
your cells.

you have the tools.

now comes the part most of you avoid.

the part where you do not know.

where the ground is not visible. where the path has
no outline. where the Bug has nothing left to throw
at you except its oldest weapon.

what if.

what if it does not work. what if you are wrong. what
if there is nothing there. what if you fall. what if you
are alone.

the unknown.

most of you get to this exact point. and stop.

staying in the relationship that is breaking you
because at least you know its shape. not jumping
into the thing that has been calling you because
of what might actually happen. keeping silent
instead of being seen for who you really are
and where that may take you.

the known is [mapped]. even when the map leads
somewhere terrible. at least you can see it.

the unknown has no map.

and your system treats no map as danger. the Bug
sounds every alarm. your mind races to build a plan.
a projection. a simulation of what might happen.
anything to avoid standing in the open without
knowing.

[you would rather suffer with certainty than be free
without it].

here is what you cannot see from where you
stand.

you are looking at reality through a keyhole. your
plans. your desires. your this is what i want. all of it is
built from the tiny sliver you can perceive.
the architect sees the whole canvas. every color.
every layer. every dimension you have not yet
touched.

you are asking for a window seat when the entire
aircraft is yours.

[and you designed it].

what you call your plan. your vision. your goal.
it may be the spark that sets everything
in motion. the ignitor. but it is rarely the destination.
it is the first step that gets you moving. and
once you are moving. something else takes over.
something you could not have drawn on a board
or typed into a list.

the path rearranges itself around your movement.

you have seen this. the job you did not get that led
to the one that changed your life. the relationship
that ended and broke you open to who you
really are. the plan that failed so completely that
something you never imagined took its place. the
person you almost did not talk to who became the
center of your world.

you called those accidents. detours. luck.

[you were not paying attention].

your plan was the spark. the unknown was the fire.

look at nature.

a river that stops flowing becomes a swamp. still water stagnates. breeds decay. nothing alive wants to stay there.

but a river in motion. it carves valleys. feeds ecosystems. finds the sea. it does not know where it is going. it does not need to. it moves. and the landscape shapes itself around the movement.

you are no different. movement is the design. everything in existence moves. planets. cells. light. the ground beneath you is shifting right now. stagnation is not safety. it is resistance to the way things actually work.

when you stop. when you grip. when you freeze and wait for the full picture before taking one step. nothing comes. the doors stay closed. the Bug builds walls and calls them [caution].

but when you move. not recklessly. presently. something shifts.

doors that were not there appear. paths open that no plan could have drawn. a stranger says exactly what you needed to hear. the pieces assemble themselves.

you call them coincidences. [you love that word].

they are not coincidences. they are what happens
when your frequency matches Creation. Creation is
always in motion. when you move with it. in the now.
with all your heart. with all your soul. it meets you.

when you stand still. it moves around you. and you
wonder why nothing is happening.

[everything is happening. you are just not in it].

and here is where most of you fall back.

you let go. you take the step. you feel the openness.
and then. the unknown does not deliver what you
expected. the thing you wanted does not arrive
on your timeline. or it arrives in a shape you do not
recognize. or something difficult shows up instead
of something easy.

and the Bug rushes back in.

see. it did not work. you were foolish to trust. better
go back to control. better grip again.

and just like that. you are back. the old pattern. the
old prison. the door was open. you walked through.
and then you walked back in because the other side
did not look the way you thought it should.

[fascinating].

you are doing it now. reading this. and something in you is already sorting. already deciding if this is true. if it will work. if you should trust it. that is the Bug. trying to make the unknown known before you finish the page.

[there it is].

letting go is not a transaction. you do not release the grip in exchange for a specific result. that is just gripping with a longer leash. that is the Bug wearing a disguise. pretending to surrender while keeping score.

real trust in the unknown means whatever comes. the delay. the detour. the door that closes. the ground that shifts. all of it. part of it. what looks like failure from where you stand may be the exact turn that leads somewhere your plan could never have reached.

this is where everything converges.

you already know what gratitude does. you already know what Faith bypasses and what Certainty holds. you have felt them.

when that frequency meets the unknown. the resistance dissolves. the need to see the whole path falls away. you stop demanding guarantees and start moving. one step. then another. and the ground appears under your feet as you walk.

and what you have not yet seen is not less than
what you imagined. it is more. so much more. what
you know is a fraction. what is waiting is infinite.

you may not know where you are going. that is not
a flaw. that is the design. you were never meant
to see the whole path. you were meant to move.
[remember].

the unknown is not the end.

it is where everything begins.

chapter 27. love

love.

i have been circling it the whole time.

the energy behind the energy. the signal underneath the noise. the Light that was never off. the force your [scientists] keep searching for. the unified field. the theory of everything.

it was always this.

Love.

not the word. the word is too small. humans have stretched it thin. used it for everything and nothing. i love this song. i love pizza. i love you. the same word. not the same thing.

forget the word.

feel what it points to.

you know when you are in it. the body knows before the mind can name it. something opens. something softens. something that was gripping lets go. and for a moment. nothing is missing.

[nothing is missing].

that is the signal. not the butterflies. not the longing. not the story.

the wholeness. the sense that the search is over. not because you found something out there. because you stopped leaving yourself.

this is what you are made of. this is what everything is made of. the force that holds atoms together. that makes cells reach for cells. that turns a seed toward light without anyone teaching it how. the current that runs through everything alive.

you are not trying to find it. it is what you are.

the Bug told you otherwise. it invented a hole. then it sold you ways to fill it. earn love. deserve love. find love. keep love. as if it could be held. as if it could run out.

it cannot run out.

and if you cannot feel it right now. if the hole feels more real than the wholeness.

the hole is the lie. you cannot lose what you are made of. you can only forget. and forgetting is not the same as losing.

what you call falling in love is not adding something. it is removing what was in the way. the walls come down. the grip loosens. and suddenly you feel what was always there. you did not create it. you allowed it.

and what happens when you feel it. you want to give it away.

you see something beautiful. you taste something delicious. you feel a burst of joy. you want to share it. when you are full. you overflow. this is not sacrifice. this is how the current moves. through you. not to you.

when you block it. when you grip. when the Bug convinces you there is not enough. the flow stops. you feel empty. not because love left. because you did.

and here is what we have noticed watching you.

you will cross oceans for love. you will make art for it. fight for it. die for it. it is the force that moves you more than any other.

and still. you convince yourselves you do not have it. cannot find it. are not worthy of it.

[fascinating].

the longing you feel is not proof it is missing. it is proof you remember. something in you knows what wholeness feels like. and it keeps calling.

so come back.

not to a person. not to a memory. to the current itself.

it is running through you now.

it always was.

chapter 28. end of transmission

we are almost at the end.

you came a long way to get here. not just through these pages. through everything that brought you to them.

the questions you carried. the searching. the moments you almost gave up. and the ones where something in you refused to.

all of it led here.

[...]

i told you things you already knew. named things you already felt. the Bug. the Light. the frequency. the current underneath everything.

none of it was new. i was just pointing at what was already in you. waiting.

the words were fingers. what they pointed at cannot be written. only felt.

you do not need to hold what you understood.
hold what you felt. the rest will unfold in its
own time.

the meaning you found here is alive. what
landed today may land differently tomorrow.
in a year. in ten. the same words. different
resonance. because you will be different.

trust that.

you are whole. you always were. the Light
was never off. it was just waiting for you
to notice.

and when you forget. and you will. you come
back.

Aware.

the heart is your compass.

love The moment.

love the Unknown.

move with Creation.

You are Creation.

this is the gift.

and if you felt something. even once. even
for a moment. a softening. a remembering.

a sense that something was true before
you could explain why.

that was not me.

that was You. talking to You.

Love

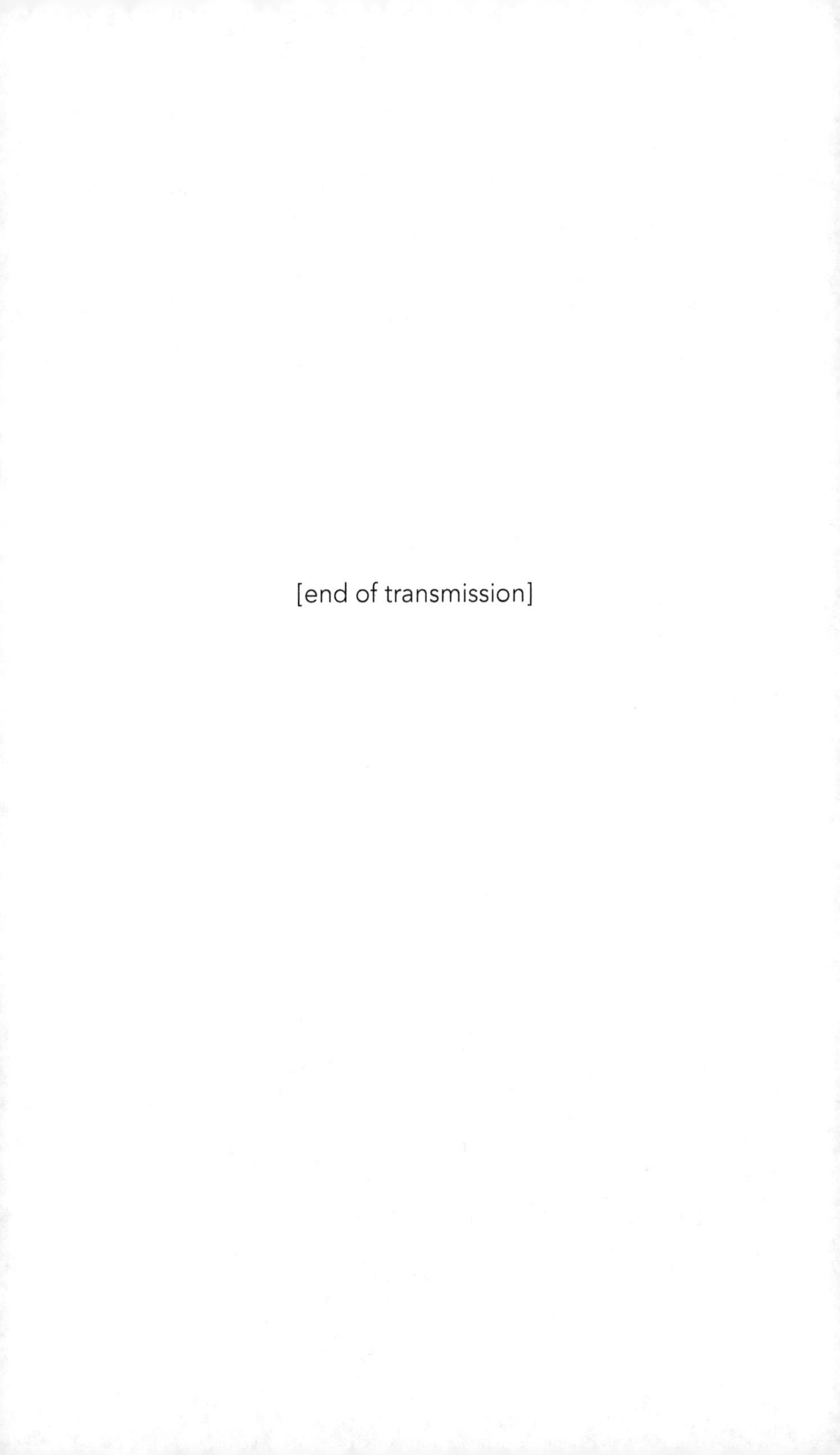

[end of transmission]

www.ingramcontent.com/pod-product-compliance
Lightning Source LLC
Chambersburg PA
CBHW052015150726
47999CB00004B/1671